Living on a
Caribbean Island

Louise and Richard Spilsbury

Raintree

www.raintreepublishers.co.uk
Visit our website to find out more information about **Raintree** books.

To order:
☎ Phone 44 (0) 1865 888112
🖹 Send a fax to 44 (0) 1865 314091
🖥 Visit the Raintree bookshop at **www.raintreepublishers.co.uk** to browse our catalogue and order online.

First published in Great Britain by
Raintree, Halley Court, Jordan Hill,
Oxford OX2 8EJ, part of Pearson Education.
Raintree is a registered trademark
of Pearson Education Ltd.

© Pearson Education Ltd 2008
First published in paperback in 2009
The moral right of the proprietor has been asserted.

Editorial: Catherine Veitch
Design: Richard Parker and Manhattan Design
Illustration: International Mapping
Picture Research: Hannah Taylor and Maria Joannou
Production: Alison Parsons

Originated by Modern Age
Printed and bound in China by CTPS

ISBN 978-1 4062 0828 3 (hardback)
12 11 10 09 08
10 9 8 7 6 5 4 3 2 1

ISBN 978-1 4062 0838 2 (paperback)
13 12 11 10 09
10 9 8 7 6 5 4 3 2 1

**British Library Cataloguing in
Publication Data**
Spilsbury, Louise and Richard
Living on a Caribbean island. - (World cultures)
972.9'053
A full catalogue record for this book is available
from the British Library.

Acknowledgements
The publishers would like to thank the following for
permission to reproduce photographs: Alamy Images
pp. **23** (Donald Nausbaum), **5** (Oliver Benn), **8** (Sylvia
Cordaiy Photo Library Ltd); Art Directors & Trip/ Paul
Joynson-hicks p. **25**; Corbis pp. **22** (Blaine Harrington
III), **12** (Bob Krist), **15** (Christian Liewig/ Liewig Media
Sports), **10** (David Cumming; Eye Ubiquitous), **21** (Peter
Turnley), **7** (Philippe Giraud); Harcourt Education Ltd/
Devon Olugbena Shaw p. **14**; Getty Images/ Stone/ Matt
Henry Gunther p. **4**; Harcourt Education Ltd/ Tudor
Photography pp. **26, 27** (top and bottom); Nature Picture
Library/ Jane Burton p. **11**; Panos Pictures pp **13** (Duncan
Simpson), **19** (Rob Huibers); Photographers Direct/
Wandering Spirit Travel Images p. **24**; Photolibrary/
Animals Animals/ Earth Scenes p. **20**; Photolibrary/ Bill
Bachmann Photography p. **18**; Robert Harding Picture
Library pp. **9** (James Gritz), **28** (Reinhard Dirscherl), **17**
(Sergio Pitamitz); Still Pictures/ Achim Pohl p. **16**; World
Pictures p. **29**.

Cover photograph of young woman in costume,
celebrating carnival, reproduced with permission of
Corbis/ Blaine Harrington III.

Carnival headdress pp. 26–27 devised and made by
Natalie Abadzis.

The publishers would like to thank Gwyneth Harold for
her assistance with the preparation of this book.

Contents

Some words are printed in bold, **like this**. You can find out what they mean on page 31.

Caribbean islands

There are many beautiful islands spread across the clear Caribbean Sea. Islands are areas of land surrounded by water. In the Caribbean one group of islands form the country of Guadeloupe (see map on page six).

◀ This Caribbean family lives in Guadeloupe. Like most people in Guadeloupe they are Creole people.

CARIBS

Caribs are the tribe (group) of people who first settled in the Caribbean. The Caribbean Sea is named after them.

Island history

Many different people have lived on Guadeloupe. The first people came from South America 1,000 years ago. People from France arrived about 500 years ago. France still rules Guadeloupe. The French brought **slaves** from Africa to work for them. Slaves are people with no freedom. Later Chinese and Indian people also came here.

Creoles are related to the different people who lived on Guadeloupe in the past. Some Creole families have left the islands and moved to other countries, such as the United States.

◀ Many Creole families in Guadeloupe grow bananas. They are sold to people in other countries.

Tropical world

Guadeloupe and the other Caribbean islands are **tropical**. Tropical places always have hot weather.

Island life

Plants grow well in tropical places. The tall trees are filled with birds and insects. Coconut palm trees grow on sandy beaches. Colourful fish swim around **coral reefs**. Coral reefs are rock-like structures in the sea. They are built by small animals called corals.

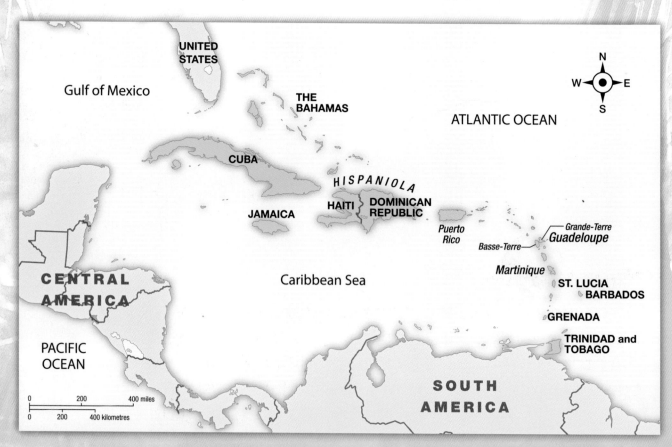

▲ The Caribbean islands make a curved line. The Caribbean Sea lies between this curve and the coasts of Central and South America.

Guadeloupe islands

Guadeloupe is made up of nine islands. The biggest are Basse-Terre and Grande-Terre. Basse-Terre is a hilly island. It was formed from rock that came out of underwater **volcanoes**! Grande-Terre is a flat island. It was made from enormous, ancient coral reefs.

▶ Hurricanes can blow down houses and trees. They sometimes hurt people.

Hurricane season

There are two seasons in the Caribbean. It is dry from February to June. From July to January it rains. **Hurricanes** often happen in September. These powerful storms blow across the Caribbean islands. People on Guadeloupe and other Caribbean islands prepare for hurricanes. They get their boats out of the water and take shelter away from the coast.

7

Many **Creoles** on Guadeloupe live in villages. Their homes are square **bungalows**. The windows have shutters with slats. These keep the rooms cool. Many bungalows are made of concrete. This stops them from blowing down in **hurricanes**.

Inside and out

Creole homes are simple. Most have a stove, a TV, a radio, and a refrigerator. Outside there is a yard where people grow fruits, herbs, and other plants. Some people keep hens to lay eggs.

◄ Many Guadeloupe houses are painted in bright, cheerful colours.

Around the village

Many villages were built around old **plantations**. Plantations are farms where plants, such as bananas and sugar, grow. Each village has a church and a school. There is often a grand stone house, where a rich landowner would have lived.

Today, many visitors come to the islands. New hotels have been built for them to stay in.

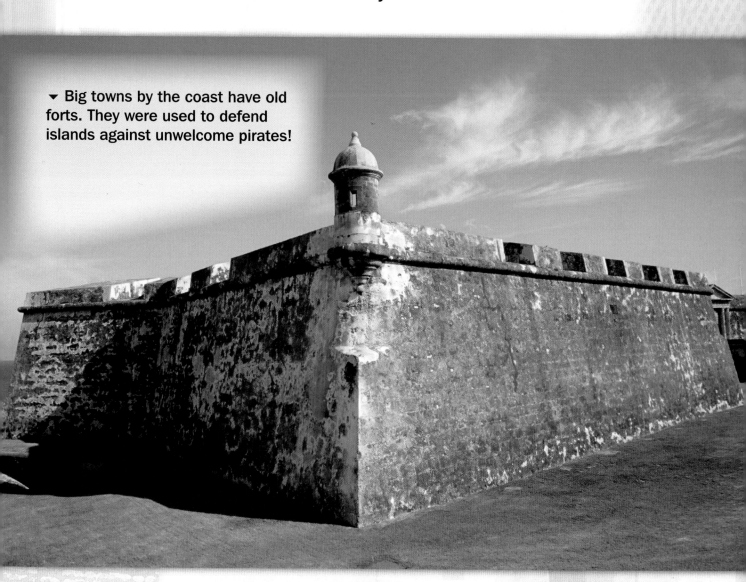

▼ Big towns by the coast have old forts. They were used to defend islands against unwelcome pirates!

Dinner time!

Creole food is a delicious mixture of tastes. These come from all over the world!

Traditional foods

Most foods are grown on the islands. People cook and mash local vegetables, such as **cassava** and **yam**. They flavour food with spices from the forest. They drink juices from guava and pineapple fruits.

Creole people also eat seafood. They barbecue fish, such as red snapper, on an open fire. They also cook fish in milk taken from coconuts. They eat the meat of giant **conches**, shellfish, and octopus.

▶ There is always a great choice of fresh, local fruit and vegetables at markets in Guadeloupe.

▲ People catch land crabs to eat. They hunt at night by shining torches at them. This blinds the crab for a moment so they can pick it up.

International meals

The people who settled in Guadeloupe brought foods from their countries. French people brought croissant pastries. Indians brought spices. Today, a curry called chicken colombo is one of the national dishes.

Now, you can even buy burgers and pizza from fast food cafés.

The community

Each **Creole** family is different. Sometimes children, parents, and grandparents live together. Other children live just with their mother. In every family, the people always help each other out.

Work

Many people work on their own farms or on bigger **plantations**. They grow fruit, coffee, cocoa, or spices. Others work in factories where fruits are packaged in bottles or cans. Some people work on mines in the hills or on fish farms near the coast.

People also find work in hotels and restaurants. They make souvenirs for tourists or take them on boat trips. Some tourists dive and snorkel round the **coral reefs**.

▲ Many tourists come to the Caribbean. They enjoy the warm, sunny weather, the beautiful beaches, and the tasty food.

▶ Lots of Caribbean people go to church. They get dressed up every Sunday.

WORSHIP

African **slaves** were brought to the Caribbean. Europeans made them pray at **Christian** churches. Their **descendants** were also taught to be Christians. Descendants are a person's children, grandchildren, and younger relatives.

Getting together

Whenever people meet in Guadeloupe, they shake hands. They also kiss each other on the cheeks.

Women often chat at the market. They go there to sell the food they grow. Men may play dominoes together. Many people also meet at the beach. On Sunday, families gather in church.

▲ The town square is a favourite meeting place. It is often bustling with people. These boys are playing dominoes.

◄ People talking on island radio stations speak in *patois*.

Creole languages

The main language in many Caribbean islands is French. School lessons are taught in French. Signposts across the islands are also in French. But most **Creole** people talk to each other in *patois*. *Patois* is a mix of European and African languages.

Patois changes from island to island. The *patois* spoken on Guadeloupe sounds different to the *patois* on the island of Jamaica.

ISLAND RADIO

The different islands can be far apart. People listen to radio stations to find out what's happening. They hear island news shows and interviews with local people. Other stations play music by Creole musicians.

15

Dressing up

Creole people wear clothes that help them stay cool. They wear T-shirts and shorts or skirts. They often wear flip-flops on their feet.

▶ Most Creole children wear uniforms for school, but they wear what they like in the evenings and at the weekend.

FLAG IT UP!

Many Caribbean people proudly wear clothes in the colours of their flag. The Jamaican flag is black, gold, and green. Grenada's flag is red, green, and gold.

Traditional costume

Slaves used to wear fancy outfits to celebrate major holidays. Women wore bright, colourful skirts with white shirts. They also wore headscarves folded into special shapes. These **traditional** clothes are still worn at festivals and celebrations today.

After slavery was banned, Indian people came to the islands. They brought checked cotton. This material is also popular in island costumes.

▲ Creole women can tie their colourful headscarves on in many different ways.

At school

On Guadeloupe all children must go to school from the age of six to seventeen. Most schools start and finish early. This means that children can learn before the hottest time of the day.

▶ Even the school uniforms are colourful in Guadeloupe!

School subjects

Children learn the usual school subjects, such as history, maths, science, and languages. Many also have lessons in dance and drama. They learn **traditional** dances such as the *quadrille*. *Quadrille* was originally a French dance. Children also learn dances that are used at carnivals.

◂ Creole children rehearse a song and dance that they will perform at the end of term.

SPEAKING

Creole children learn French at school. This can make it easier for them to get jobs in future. Some teachers speak ***patois*** to make sure children can understand them.

Time out!

Caribbean people do lots of fun outdoor activities. They have barbecues on beaches and play games, such as volleyball. Around Easter time, most islanders in Guadeloupe watch the annual football match against Martinique. Martinique is a neighbouring island (see map on page six).

▲ There's so much to do living by the Caribbean Sea. People can swim, snorkel, surf, or go boating.

▶ Modern Caribbean music is a mixture of sounds and rhythms from France, England, Spain, and Africa.

PARTY!

Zouk is the **Creole** word for party. It is also a popular type of dance music in Guadeloupe. It is a mixture of *gwo ka* rhythms and rock guitar.

Music

Music fills the air in the Caribbean. One of the oldest music styles is *gwo ka*. *Gwo ka* means big drums. The drums are played in different rhythms to accompany songs.

Dancing

The limbo dance is often done for fun on the beach. People lean back and try to dance under a horizontal pole. The limbo stick reminds Creole people of the time when African **slaves** travelled to the Caribbean. The slaves came on ships and had to go down into very low holds (decks).

21

Carnival!

Nearly every Caribbean island has big carnivals. They last for days! People join in with costumed processions, dancing, feasting (eating), and fun!

◀ These children are taking part in a children's carnival.

Mardi Gras

The biggest carnival on Guadeloupe is the *Mardi Gras*. This is during the dry season, before the rains and storms come. The carnival happens in the run-up to Easter. This is an important time for **Christian** people.

Sights and sounds

Mardi Gras starts on a Sunday with a parade. For four days there are parties, dances, music, singing, and a costume competition.

The music includes **steel bands**. Steel bands are groups who play metal oil drums. The music first came from the Caribbean island of Trinidad.

The festival ends on Wednesday with the burning of *Vaval*, a giant puppet. *Vaval* is the symbol of carnival.

▶ People dress up as devils in this Easter carnival.

MIXING CULTURES

Mardi Gras brings together different **cultures**. It uses dances, costumes, and traditions from Africa. It also follows the Easter timetable. European settlers brought Easter to the islands.

Remembering the past

All Saints' Day is a **Christian** festival on 1 November. It is when **Creole** people remember their dead loved ones.

Sharing memories

On All Saints' Day, families eat special foods, such as land crab with rice. Families gather to share memories about their **ancestors**.

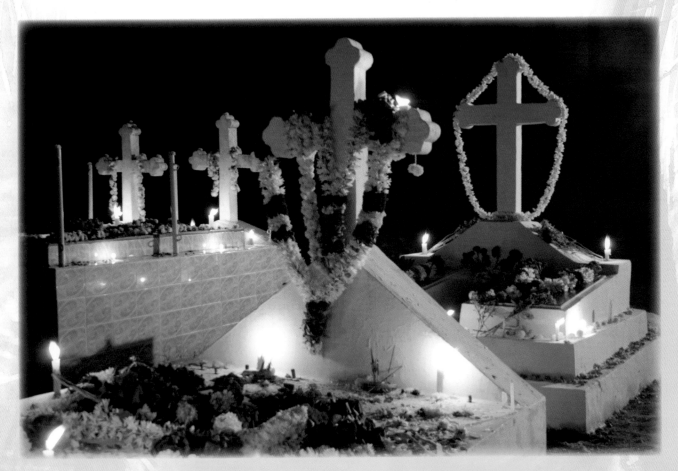

▲ Before All Saints' Day, people visit cemeteries. They clean up family burial plots. On the day, they light candles on gravestones.

Stories

In the past, storytellers travelled between villages in West Africa. They shared tales and music. Today, older people in the Caribbean tell stories in *patois* at All Saints. They also play *gwo ka* drums.

▲ Some stories are about African animals, such as monkeys and lions. Others describe events from Creole history, such as slavery.

ANANCY

Anancy (or Anansi) is a character in Caribbean stories. He first appeared in West African **slave** tales. He is sometimes a person. More often, he is a clever spider! In some stories, Anancy tricks wild animals. Other stories are about him saving slaves from danger on **plantations**.

Make a carnival headdress!

The headgear worn at carnivals is colourful and interesting. You can wear it, or use it to decorate a room!

Many types of headgear are worn at Caribbean carnivals. They all follow African traditions. They use natural objects, such as grasses, wooden beads, feathers, and shells. Feathers are often used in African masks. People believe feathers help get rid of their problems and pains.

To make a carnival headdress you will need:
- bendy A2 size coloured card
- feathers
- bobbles
- sequins
- glitter
- safe glue
- stapler
- scissors
- pencil.

Step 1

Draw a design on the card lightly in pencil. Extend the bits that will go around your head. Then cut it out. Make sure the headband fits your head and there is enough card to staple together after you have decorated it (see picture).

Step 2

Now the fun starts! Decorate your headdress with feathers, bobbles, glitter, and sequins. Ask an adult to staple the two ends together to fit the headdress around your head.

Did you know?

- Every year millions of people eat Caribbean seafood, spices, and crops from bananas to coffee.

- The Caribbean Sea and the islands are home to many different species of animals. There are turtles, crocodiles, parrots, hummingbirds, whales, dolphins, and more. There are also some of the finest **coral reefs** in the world.

- Millions of visitors from all over the world come to experience the **Creole culture**, nature, and the warm weather.

- Caribbean music is listened to around the world.

▶ Many tourists come to the Caribbean to go diving and see the colourful world beneath the waves.

Island names

Christopher Columbus (1451–1506), an Italian explorer, named Guadeloupe after a **Christian** saint. Its Carib tribe name was *Karukera*. *Karukera* means "island of beautiful waters".

Other ancient names for Caribbean islands describe what they are like. For example, *Xaymaca* (pronounced Jamaica) means "land of wood and water". This is because of the forests and rivers in Jamaica.

Lere was the early name for Trinidad. It means "land of the hummingbird". This is because lots of hummingbirds live there.

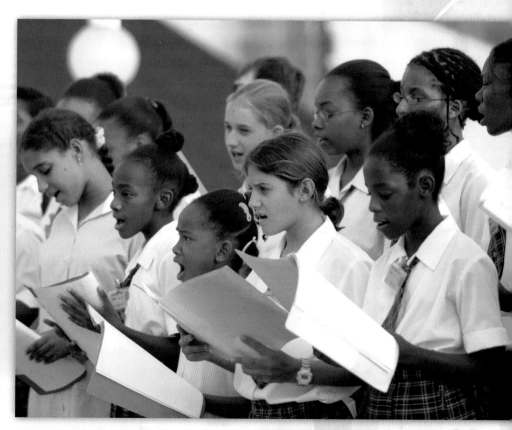

▸ The Caribbean islands are home to nearly 30 million people. The people have different backgrounds and a mix of cultures.

Find out for yourself

Books to read

Clever Anansi and Boastful Bullfrog: A Caribbean Tale, H. Patten (Frances Lincoln Publishers, 2000)

Sing Me a Story! Song and Dance Stories from the Caribbean, Grace Hallworth (Frances Lincoln Publishers, 2003)

We Come From Jamaica, Alison Brownlie (Hodder Wayland, 1999)

Websites

To read some Anancy stories look at these websites:

www.globaleye.org.uk/primary_spring04/focuson/tigerstory.html

www.manteno.k12.il.us/WebQuest/elementary/LanguageArts/Anasi/anansibookred.html

Glossary

ancestor relative, such as a great-grandparent, from a long time before

bungalow home that is built on only one level

cassava potato-like root of a plant, used in cooking and making cakes

Christian person who follows the Christian religion and believes in Jesus Christ

conch sea creature with a spiral shell

coral reef rock-like structures built by small animals called corals

Creole Caribbean people whose ancestors were European, African, or Indian

culture way of life of a society

descendant child, grandchild, great-grandchild, and so on, of a particular family

hurricane powerful, spinning wind that can cause terrible damage

patois local Caribbean language

plantation large area of land in a tropical place where crops (such as bananas or coffee) are grown

slave person who is forced to work for someone else against his or her will. Slaves are given little or no money.

steel band Caribbean music band that plays steel drums made from oil drums

traditional story or way of doing something that has been the same for many years

tropical hot area of the world near the equator (an imaginary line round the middle of the Earth)

volcano opening in the Earth's surface where melted rock pours out. It often hardens to form a cone-shaped mountain or island.

yam vegetable that grows underground in hot countries

Index